I am
Rosa Parks

BRAD MELTZER

illustrated by Christopher Eliopoulos

DIAL BOOKS FOR YOUNG READERS an imprint of Penguin Group (USA) LLC

I am **Rosa Parks.**

Growing up, I was small for my age.
I was sick a lot too, since we didn't have money for a doctor.
But that didn't mean I was weak.

When I was eleven, as I was walking home from school, a boy on roller skates came zipping by and shoved me. He thought I'd be an easy target.

To his surprise, I turned around and pushed him back. I knew fighting was wrong. But I didn't want him picking on me again.

His mother saw what happened. She was mad that I'd pushed him.

I stood my ground.
And calmly, but firmly, I explained . . .

I wasn't just standing up to that mom. Or even to the boy on roller skates.
I was standing up for myself.
After that, the boy and his mom never bothered me again.
Still, it's hard to change things. Sometimes it can take a long time.

Back then, if you were black, you were treated unfairly just because of the color of your skin.

You weren't allowed to live in the same neighborhood as a white person, eat in the same restaurant, ride the same elevator, or use the same bathroom.

You couldn't even drink from the same water fountain. One was marked for "Whites"; the other for "Colored."

When I was little, I used to wonder if "white" water tasted different from "colored" water. I even wondered if "colored" water came in lots of colors.

But it didn't.
The only difference was I had to walk outside, or even down the block, to get mine. Of course, it wasn't just about water fountains.

This was my school, a small, old wooden building with one room and one teacher . . . for *all* of us. Everyone from the five-year-olds to the sixth graders were stuffed in that one room. There were no windows, desks, and barely any books.

SINCE MOST KIDS HAD TO WORK ON A FARM TO EARN MONEY, WE ONLY WENT TO SCHOOL FIVE MONTHS DURING THE YEAR.

LESS SCHOOL! *HOORAY!*

DON'T SAY "HOORAY." THAT'S BAD.

We also brought our books home every night. Why? Because we were worried that folks who hated the color of our skin would burn down our school.

Now, here's the school for the kids who were white. Notice the difference?

It was a new brick building with beautiful windows, new desks, and plenty of books. Plus a playground.

Also, if you were black, you had to walk to school.
If you were white, you got to take a bus.

The worst part was, when I'd walk home with my brother, the kids on the bus would throw trash at us.

It made me feel horrible.

But there were no "civil rights" back then. The only solution was to move off the road.

And really, what kind of solution is that?

As I got older, things didn't change much.

One winter, I was waiting for the local city bus.
If you were black, you had to ride in the back.
If you were white, you rode up front.
On that day, the back of the bus was packed.

The driver didn't care. He wanted me off the bus.
He grabbed me by my coat sleeve.
I dropped my purse near the front door. To pick it up, I sat in the front seat—a white seat. It made the driver madder than ever.

That's what he called it.
"My bus." As if it were his.
The bus *wasn't* his, though.
It belonged to all of us.

From there, in addition to working as a seamstress, I started working to change things.

At the NAACP, we fought for fairer laws, and made sure that people's stories were heard.

I also stopped using "colored" water fountains. I'd rather go thirsty than be treated so poorly.

It was the same with separate elevators. Instead of riding them, I'd take the stairs.

But as for real change . . .

It was the end of a busy Thursday.

I was forty-two years old and on the bus, going home.

This time, I was sitting in the first row of seats that were allowed for black people.

There was one man next to me, and two women across from me.

It was the same driver from before.
The exact same one from all those years earlier.

At the third stop, a few white people got on, filling the rest of the empty seats.

There was one white person left standing, so the driver told those of us in my row . . .

Sliding over to the window, I thought about what he was demanding.

He wanted to take my seat away. He wanted to give it to that man. And why?

Because I was black . . . and the man was white.

C'MON, GET UP!

I knew what the rules said. But I also knew in my heart: That's not how you treat people.

Without a doubt, the driver was mad.
But I never lost my cool.
Never raised my voice.

People say that the reason I refused to give up my seat was because I was tired.

And I was. But it wasn't the kind of tired that came from aching feet.

The only tired I was, was tired of giving in.

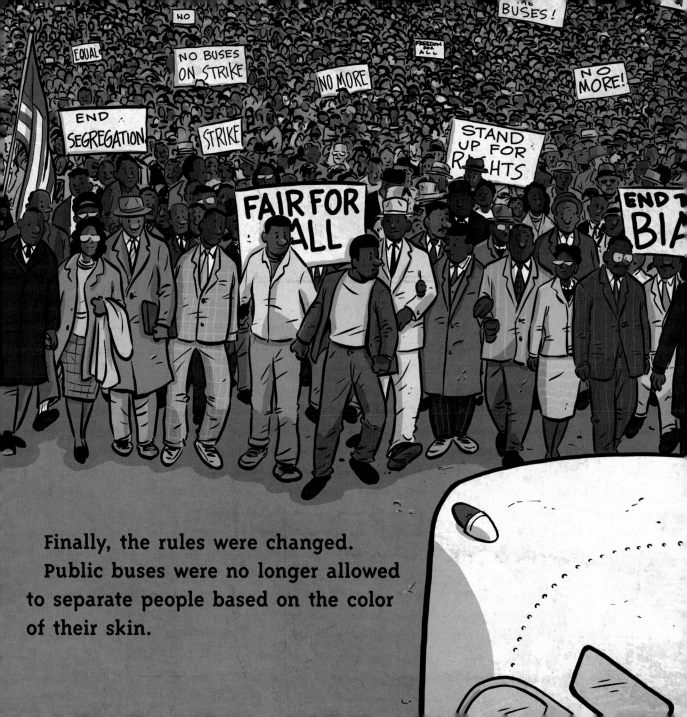

Finally, the rules were changed.
Public buses were no longer allowed
to separate people based on the color
of their skin.

That was only the beginning.

Eventually, we were allowed to drink from the same water fountains, ride the same elevators, and yes, go to the same schools.

In the Declaration of Independence, Thomas Jefferson wrote that we're all created equal.

Finally, the nation was starting to act like it.

Of course, that didn't mean the fight was over.
There were thousands of other people just like
that bus driver.

But after hearing how I didn't give up my seat,
there were now thousands more people just like me.
Together. Inspired. And committed to justice.

In my life, people tried to knock me down.
Tried to make me feel less than I was. They teased
me for being small. Being black. Being different.
Let me be clear: No one should be able to do that.

But if they try, you must stand strong.
Stand for what's right.
Stand up for yourself (even if it means sitting down).

When you do . . .

Others will follow.

I am Rosa Parks.
I'm not a politician, or a president,
or an actor, or a famous business owner.
I'm just an ordinary person.
But I'm also proof that there's *no such thing*
as an ordinary person.

I hope you'll always stand up for yourself,
and I hope you'll remember that
we're all in this together.

"The only tired I was, was tired of giving in."
—ROSA PARKS

 Timeline

FEBRUARY 4, 1913

Born in Tuskegee, Alabama

1943

Kicked off a bus for entering through the front door

DECEMBER 1943

Became secretary of the Montgomery chapter of the NAACP

DECEMBER 1, 1955

Arrested for refusing to give up her seat on the bus

Rosa's police photo, taken in 1956

Rosa after bus segregation was outlawed (1956)

A typical segregated classroom
when Rosa was young

DECEMBER 4, 1955 — Montgomery Bus Boycott announced

DECEMBER 17, 1956 — U.S. Supreme Court rules that bus segregation is unconstitutional

1979 — Received the Spingarn Medal, the NAACP's highest honor

1992 — Published her autobiography, *Rosa Parks: My Story*

1999 — Received the Congressional Gold Medal

OCTOBER 24, 2005 — Died at age 92 in Detroit, Michigan

In memory of
Dotty Rubin,
my Nanny and Grandmother,
who loved her family,
loved her politics,
and always fought for the right side
—B.M.

For my mother, Sandy,
who taught me to treat everyone equally
and gave me my love of history
—C.E.

For historical accuracy, we tried to use Rosa's and the bus driver's actual dialogue. For more of Rosa's true voice, we recommend and acknowledge the autobiography *Rosa Parks: My Story* (see below).

SOURCES
Rosa Parks: My Story by Rosa Parks with Jim Haskins (Dial Books, 1992)
Rosa Parks by Douglas Brinkley (Viking, 2000)
Rosa Parks: Civil Rights Leader by Mary Hull (Chelsea House, 2006)
The Rebellious Life of Mrs. Rosa Parks by Jeanne Theoharis (Beacon Press, 2013)
Don't Know Much About Rosa Parks by Kenneth C. Davis (HarperCollins, 2005)

FURTHER READING FOR KIDS
Rosa by Nikki Giovanni (Henry Holt, 2005)
Back of the Bus by Aaron Reynolds (Philomel, 2010)
I Am Rosa Parks by Rosa Parks (Penguin Young Readers, 1997)
Who Was Rosa Parks? by Yona Zeldis McDonough (Grosset, 2010)

DIAL BOOKS FOR YOUNG READERS
Published by the Penguin Group • Penguin Group (USA) LLC, 375 Hudson Street, New York, New York 10014

USA | Canada | UK | Ireland | Australia | New Zealand | India | South Africa | China
penguin.com

A PENGUIN RANDOM HOUSE COMPANY

Text copyright © 2014 by Forty-four Steps, Inc • Illustrations copyright © 2014 by Christopher Eliopoulos

Library of Congress Cataloging-in-Publication Data. • Meltzer, Brad. • I am Rosa Parks / Brad Meltzer ; illustrated by Christopher Eliopoulos. • pages cm. — (Ordinary people change the world).
ISBN 978-0-8037-4085-3 (hardcover) • 1. Parks, Rosa, 1913–2005—Juvenile literature. 2. African American women—Alabama—Montgomery—Biography—Juvenile literature. 3. African Americans—Alabama—Montgomery—Biography—Juvenile literature. 4. Civil rights workers—Alabama—Montgomery—Biography—Juvenile literature. 5. African Americans—Civil rights—Alabama—Montgomery—History—20th century—Juvenile literature. 6. Segregation in transportation—Alabama—Montgomery—History—20th century—Juvenile literature. 7. Montgomery (Ala.)—Race relations—Juvenile literature. 8. Montgomery (Ala.)—Biography—Juvenile literature. I. Eliopoulos, Christopher, illustrator. II. Title. F334.M753P385554 2014 323.092—dc23 [B] 2013034308

Rosa Parks photograph on page 38 courtesy of the Johnson Publishing Company, LLC. Photograph of Rosa sitting on the bus on page 39 courtesy of Corbis.
Rosa Parks mug shot on page 39 courtesy of the Associated Press. Segregated classroom photograph on page 39 courtesy of the Library of Congress.

Manufactured in China on acid-free paper • 10 9 8 7 6 5 4 3
Designed by Jason Henry • Text set in Triplex • The artwork for this book was created digitally.